MICHAEL JORDAN

BASKETBALL TO BASEBALL AND BACK

REVISED EDITION
BY BILL GUTMAN

Millbrook Sports World
The Millbrook Press
Brookfield, Connecticut

Photographs courtesy of Focus on Sports: cover, cover inset; John W. McDonough: pp. 3, 4, 46; North Hanover Public Library, Cape Fear Tidewater Collection: pp. 6, 7, 10; AP/Wide World Photos: pp. 13, 16, 19, 20, 37, 42, 44; Bill Smith: pp. 23, 26, 29; Sports Illustrated: p. 34 (Manny Millan), 39 (Walter Ioss, Jr.).

Library of Congress Cataloging-in-Publication Data
Gutman, Bill.
Michael Jordan : basketball to baseball and back / by Bill Gutman. — Rev. ed.
p. cm. — (Millbrook sports world)
Includes index.
Summary: Examines the personal life and basketball career of the high-scoring player with the Chicago Bulls, who made a brief attempt to play minor league baseball in 1994.
ISBN 1-56294-924-1 (lib. bdg.) ISBN 1-56294-902-0 (pbk.)
1. Jordan, Michael, 1963- —Juvenile literature. 2. Basketball players—United States—Biography—Juvenile literature.
[1. Jordan, Michael, 1963- . 2. Basketball players. 3. Afro-Americans—Biography.] I. Title. II. Series.
GV884.J67G876 1995
796.323′092—dc20
[B]   95-19671   CIP   AC

Published by The Millbrook Press, Inc.
2 Old New Milford Road
Brookfield, Connecticut

MICHAEL JORDAN

In March 1982, the University of North Carolina and Georgetown University played the biggest college basketball game of the year—for the National Championship. Both teams had star players. Georgetown had center Patrick Ewing and guard Eric "Sleepy" Floyd. North Carolina had forward James Worthy and center Sam Perkins. All four were All-Americans and would become outstanding pros. But when the game ended, it was another player who would stand out.

Nineteen-year-old North Carolina freshman Michael Jordan had won a starting guard spot on the team at the beginning of the year. Yet most people didn't know how good he really was. They soon found out.

The game was very close from start to finish. With just 15 seconds left, Georgetown had a one-point lead, 62-61, but North Carolina had the ball. As the clock ticked down, Michael Jordan got the ball on the left baseline about 16 feet (4.88 meters) from the basket.

Starting with his years at Laney High, then at the University of North Carolina, and finally with the Chicago Bulls, Michael Jordan has been soaring over opponents and scoring baskets in gravity-defying ways.

Michael didn't try to pass the ball to one of his well-known teammates. Instead, he leaped into the air and took his jump shot. Thousands of fans around the country held their breaths. The ball dropped through the net.

Michael was a happy kid who enjoyed being with his family and growing up in Wilmington, North Carolina.

Michael Jordan made the winning basket and became the biggest hero in North Carolina.

That was only the beginning. Before long, people were lining up to watch Michael play basketball. They were amazed each time they saw him. Michael could do things on the court that no player before him had ever been able to do. Because he could jump so high, his nickname was "Air Jordan." And in the minds of many, he was the most talented player ever.

THE EARLY YEARS

Michael Jordan was born in Brooklyn, New York, on February 17, 1963. Soon after he was born, his parents decided to move their family to Wilmington, North Carolina. Wilmington wasn't at all like Brooklyn or New York City. In the 1960s, Wilmington was a sleepy southern town. It didn't have the hustle and bustle of a big city. There was also less of a drug and crime problem. James and Delores Jordan felt that Wilmington would be a good place to raise children.

The Jordans taught their children the value of hard work. James worked at a General Electric plant where he became a supervisor. Delores found a job at a bank. She became head of customer relations.

"We always tried to make things happen," James said. "We didn't wait around for them to happen to us. If you work hard you will get the things you want."

Michael spent his childhood playing all the different sports with his friends. None of the men in the Jordan

Baseball was Michael's early love when it came to sports. Notice the determined look in his eyes as he gets set to bat during a Little League game in Wilmington. He was a pitcher and outfielder and continued to play the game right into high school.

family were over 6 feet (183 centimeters) tall, so as a young boy Michael did not even think about becoming a basketball player.

For a while, he played a lot of baseball. In fact, when he was 12 years old, he was named the best baseball player in his league. His picture in the local newspaper showed a very thin boy with big ears.

Michael went to D.C. Virgo Junior High School in Wilmington when he was 13. By that time, he was playing football, basketball, and baseball. He was a good all-around athlete.

"Michael always hated losing," said Fred Lynch, who was Michael's coach in junior high and later an assistant coach where Michael went to high school. "That always made him work harder. He also had a great deal of support from his parents. They came to all the games and always found a way to praise him, no matter how the game ended."

He developed yet another habit early in life. During tense moments, Michael would stick his tongue out of his mouth. His father did the same thing while working in their garage. Michael's coaches told him it was dangerous because he could accidentally bite his tongue. But Michael couldn't stop doing it. This quirk would become a trademark.

HIGH SCHOOL STANDOUT

Michael was 5 feet 10 inches (178 centimeters) tall when he entered Laney High School as a tenth grader in the fall of 1978. When he first went to Laney, Michael was still playing three sports. He became the starting point guard with the JV basketball squad and had a good year. Toward the end of the season the coach took a taller player to join the varsity for the state championship tournament. Not being picked was something Michael would never forget.

"I made up my mind right then and there that this would never happen to me again," Michael said. "From that point on, I began working harder than ever on my basketball skills."

Michael began practicing as much as he could. In fact, he started cutting classes to spend more time in the gym. Finally he was suspended from school. When he came back he did the same thing again and was suspended a second time. After three suspensions, his father stepped in.

"I asked Michael if he wanted to go to college," James said. "When he said yes I told him there was no way it was going to happen, not the way he was cutting classes."

That woke Michael up.

"I knew my father was right," he said. "I would just have to find better times to practice basketball. I always said I was lucky to have parents who cared."

After that, Michael stopped skipping classes. Then when he returned for his junior year, Michael surprised everyone. People had to look twice at him, because he had suddenly grown a full 5 inches (12.7 centimeters). He was now 6 feet 3 inches (191 centimeters) tall. Even his father was surprised it had happened so fast.

"It was almost as if Michael willed himself taller," James said.

Michael had already given up football to get ready for basketball season. After his junior year he stopped playing baseball, too. Then it was just basketball and more basketball.

He found he could practice with both the junior varsity and varsity and not miss any classes.

"Michael was very coachable in high school," said Fred Lynch. "But he always demanded the other players go as hard as he did. He was a pusher because he hated to lose. Yet he never blamed teammates if things didn't go well. That wasn't his style."

A family portrait, taken when Michael was about 11 years old. Standing behind his parents, Delores and James, Michael is the third child from the left.

Michael's style was simply outstanding basketball. He could always jump higher than most of his teammates. Now he was starting to drive to the hoop. He would twist and turn in midair, faking one, two, even three times. Then he would put the ball in the basket.

The summer between his junior and senior years Michael went to the Five-Star Basketball Camp in Pittsburgh. Only the best high school players in the country were invited. As soon as Michael started playing, he amazed everyone.

"The first time Michael took a jump shot he got up so high it was like there was no defender," one of the coaches said. "It was like he was playing a different game."

There was little doubt now that Michael was good enough to play college basketball. He still had another year at Laney High. But people were already wondering which college he would attend.

Michael visited the University of North Carolina at Chapel Hill and liked what he saw. He made up his mind almost immediately. In the fall of 1981, he would go to the University of North Carolina.

As a high school senior in 1980, Michael was almost 6 feet 5 inches (196 centimeters) tall. He worked as hard as ever, not letting up for a second. For the season he averaged 27.8 points and 12 rebounds a game. That was almost a point a minute in a 32-minute high school game.

Michael remained a popular student at Laney High. His friends called him Mike, and he was friendly to everyone. His high school years were very happy. After he stopped cutting classes for basketball, Michael became a good student and graduated in June 1981.

FRESHMAN TAR HEEL

Dean Smith was the basketball coach at North Carolina. He was one of the best in the country. Throughout the years, the North Carolina team, called the Tar Heels, had always won a lot of games. But the team had won the national championship only once. That was back in 1957.

Now there were a number of very good players returning for the 1981-1982 season. Both James Worthy and Sam Perkins were potential All-Americans. What the team needed, however, was a player to start at shooting guard. That was the spot Michael Jordan wanted.

In a pickup game with his new teammates, he shocked everyone by scoring the winning basket on an incredible slam dunk over 7-footer (213-centimeter) Geoff Compton.

"When I made my move . . . I wound up going over two players, and dunked," Michael remembered. "When I came down to the floor I said to myself, 'Was that me?'"

Michael was eager to learn and blend in with his new teammates right away. Then, just before the first game, Coach Smith named him the fifth starter.

"I didn't know I'd be starting until I saw my name on the board," Michael said. "And believe me, I was nervous."

North Carolina's first game was against Kansas. Michael scored his team's first two points and played well. When the game ended, North Carolina had won, 74-67, and Michael had 12 points. In his third game he scored more than 20 points for the first time. The Tar Heels went on to win their first ten games and were ranked as the number one team in the country.

Next the team played a big game against the University of Virginia and their star center, 7-foot-4 (224-centimeter) Ralph Sampson. The Cavaliers and Tar Heels were the two best teams in the Atlantic Coast Conference (ACC).

As a freshman at the University of North Carolina, Michael made the last-second shot that won the national championship for the Tar Heels. As an encore, he became Player of the Year the following two seasons. Here he drives around Clemson's Marc Campbell during the Atlantic Coast Conference tournament in 1983.

It was a tough, close game, but North Carolina won it, 65-60. Michael scored 16 points and hit 5 of his 7 shots in the second half. As usual, North Carolina had balanced scoring. Coach Smith liked it that way. He didn't feel that any one player should score the majority of the points.

When the regular season ended, the Tar Heels had lost just two games and were ACC champs. Then they won the ACC tournament, beating Virginia again, 47-45, in the title game. Michael hit four straight jump shots in the final minutes to help his team win. North Carolina was now the top-ranked team in the country and the favorite to win the NCAA tournament.

Sure enough, they made it to the title game against the Hoyas of Georgetown. Michael hit the winning shot in this game with just 15 seconds left. It gave his team the championship and made him the biggest hero in the state of North Carolina. Michael wound up with 16 points in the final game. His average for his freshman season was 13.5 points a game, and he helped his team to a great 32-2 season.

He was the only freshman to make the all-tournament team. But what people remembered most was his winning basket. From that day on, everyone in North Carolina knew what was meant by "the shot."

PLAYER OF THE YEAR

In spite of his fame, Michael didn't get a swelled head. He always tried to keep up with his schoolwork and old friends even though the game took up a lot of his time.

"I'm the same person I always was," he said. "I try to write and call and stay in touch with all the people I knew before."

Michael's roommate, Buzz Peterson, was also on the basketball team. The two became very good friends and set an example in brotherhood for everyone. Michael, of course, was black and Buzz Peterson was white. But that didn't matter to either of them.

"What impressed me about Michael was his love for his parents and his family," Peterson said. "He was also a fun guy to be around, except when he was on the basketball court. Then he became deadly serious."

The Tar Heels didn't have James Worthy playing in 1982-1983. He had gone to the pros. Now the team needed Michael to score more. He had 32 points against Duke, then scored 39 against Georgia Tech. As usual, he was at his best at "crunch time," the last few minutes of a close game. That's when he always wanted the ball.

North Carolina finished the year with a 28-8 record. They didn't win the national championship, but they were still a good team. Michael averaged 20 points a game and was named to every All-American team. Better yet, after the season ended, he was named College Basketball's Player of the Year. It is the highest honor a player can receive.

But the day after the final game of the season Michael was in the gym again. Practicing—and practicing some more. He told his friends he "couldn't wait for the next game."

At the beginning of his junior season, Michael put a lot of pressure on himself to carry the team. He had never done that before. As a result, he didn't play well at first. His father told him to just settle down. "Play like Michael Jordan," he said, "and things will fall into place."

That's what Michael did. In a game against Louisiana State University he had 23 points in the second half alone. He had taken control of the game

and once again looked like the best college player in the country. With Michael leading the way, North Carolina finished the regular season at 27-2. They won the ACC title for the third straight time. But then they were upset by Indiana in the second round of the NCAA tournament.

It had still been a great year. Michael averaged 19.6 points for the season, and in the final 10 games his average was 24.1. His overall game had improved and he had worked hard to make himself an outstanding defensive player, too. For his efforts, he was named Player of the Year for the second straight time.

"Making the crowd and my teammates happy makes me happy," Michael said. "I love the game, I really do. I never think of it as a job."

But now Michael had a big decision to make. He had one more year at North Carolina. He was a geography major and felt he should get his degree. He also felt he owed the team another year. But Coach Smith thought he was ready for the pros.

"The coach felt Michael could make a lot of money and should get started on his pro career," said assistant coach Bill Guthridge.

On May 5, 1984, Michael made his announcement. "I have to do what's best for me. I feel I owe it to my parents who have put up with me for 20 years. I want the chance to move up to a higher level and make a better life for myself. So I'm going to turn pro."

Michael collected a lot of trophies after his junior year season of 1983-1984. He was college basketball's Player of the Year for the second straight season and also won the Eastman Award, given to the top male collegiate hoopster. Here, a smiling and dapper Michael proudly displays the Eastman trophy.

ROOKIE OF THE YEAR

In the summer of 1984, Michael made the United States Olympic Basketball team. He played brilliantly and helped the U.S. team win a gold medal. By the time the Olympics ended, the NBA draft had been held, and Michael learned he was the third player taken after centers Hakeem Olajuwon and Sam Bowie.

The team that drafted Michael was the Chicago Bulls. In the two seasons before picking Michael the Bulls had records of 28-54 and 27-55. They hadn't made the play-offs either time. But the Bulls had high hopes for Michael. They signed him to a contract worth $6.15 million for seven years. At the time it was one of the biggest contracts ever given to a rookie.

Kevin Loughery, the Bulls coach in 1984-1985, decided right away to turn Michael loose. He told his rookie to score any way he wanted. He wouldn't ask him to stay within a set system, as had been the case at North Carolina.

The rest of the league soon found out they had a tiger by the tail. Michael was nearly unstoppable. Sometimes he used his speed to blow past veteran players. Or he used his jumping ability to soar over them. He could fake two or three times while in the air, then make a great shot. Not many players could do that.

Michael didn't even need time to adjust to the tougher brand of NBA play. In just his third game he erupted for 37 points against Milwaukee. Then

Before joining the Chicago Bulls, Michael was part of the 1984 U.S. Olympic basketball team. His outstanding play helped the United States win a gold medal. Here Michael goes up for two points in a 97-49 rout of China in a game played at the Forum in Los Angeles.

in the Bulls' ninth game, he scored 45 points in a victory over San Antonio. And he was scoring from every spot on the court.

"I never practice the fancy stuff," Michael explained. "If I thought about a move, I'd probably turn the ball over. I just look at a situation in the air, adjust, create, and let instinct take over."

By midseason, Michael was named to the Eastern Division All-Star squad and was battling the New York Knicks' Bernard King for the scoring lead. In addition, he was leading the Bulls in scoring, rebounding, assists, steals, and minutes played. Fans in all the league cities were flocking to see him whenever the Bulls came to town.

He was also beginning to lend his nickname to products. The "Air Jordan" sneaker quickly became the hottest seller on the market. His quick smile and deep baritone voice made him perfect for commercials.

After the All-Star game, Michael was even better. He had one stretch of games in which he scored 42, 36, 35, 45, 38, 41, and 49 points. There wasn't a player in the league who could really stop him on defense.

At the end of the season, the Bulls' record had improved to 38-44, and they made the play-offs for the first time since 1981. As for Michael, he scored a team record of 2,313 points, good for a 28.2 average. Bernard King won the scoring title with a 32.9 average, but played in just 55 games before being hurt. So Michael had the most points in the league. He then averaged 29.3 in four play-off games against the Milwaukee Bucks, even though the Bulls lost.

In September 1984, Michael signed a seven-year contract with the Chicago Bulls that made him the third-highest-paid rookie in NBA history. He would prove he was worth every penny and more as he became a superstar from his first day as a pro.

When the year ended, Air Jordan was on the All-Eastern Division first team. He was also named Schick Pivotal Player of the Year and the Seagram's NBA Player of the Year. Then both the *Sporting News* and the NBA named him Rookie of the Year.

BUILDING A WINNER

The 1985–1986 season wasn't easy for Michael. In the third game of his second season he went up for one of his slam-dunks. But this time he didn't land right. The result was a broken bone in his left foot. It was the first bad injury he ever had.

It was hard for Michael to sit out the game he loved so much. Although the cast came off his foot in December, it wasn't healing fast enough. The doctors told him to wait, but Michael went back to the University of North Carolina and began practicing on his own.

"The toughest part was mental," Michael said. "I thought I might be making a mistake, but as I ran the court I couldn't feel anything wrong. When I finally dunked the ball, it felt just wonderful."

The Bulls wanted Michael to sit out the entire year, but he wanted to test the foot. Finally, near the end of the season, he got back in. In his first game back he dunked over 7-foot-3 (221-centimeter) Randy Breuer of the Bucks. That's when he knew he was fine.

With his foot in a cast, Michael still stayed close to his teammates. He often hobbled to the games on crutches and watched from the bench. Once the cast was off, however, he went home to North Carolina and began practicing in earnest.

Because of the injury, Michael played in only 18 games in 1985-1986 and averaged just 22.7 points a contest. The Bulls, however, made the play-offs despite a 30-52 record. They then lost to the Boston Celtics in the first round, 3-0. But Michael was ready to play full-time, and in the first game against the Celtics soared for 49 points. Then in the next he got 63 in double overtime. Even though Boston won, Michael showed everyone he was more than back. He was better than ever and ready to fly.

Healthy again, Michael wanted to help build a winning team. But in 1986–1987 there just weren't enough good players. In the first game of the season, Michael went out and scored 50 points against the New York Knicks. He looked great, and continued to look great all year.

When it ended, Michael had won his first scoring title with a 37.1 average. He scored 3,041 points, making him the only NBA player besides the legendary Wilt Chamberlain to score more than 3,000 points in a season. He was also the first player ever to have more than 200 steals and 100 blocks in the same year. But the team was only 40-42 and lost again to the Celtics in the play-offs.

In 1987-1988, the Bulls drafted a pair of young forwards, 6-foot-7 (201-centimeter) Scottie Pippen and 6-foot-10 (208-centimeter) Horace Grant. Neither was an instant star, but both had talent. And Air Jordan had his finest season ever. The improvement showed in the team record. The Bulls finished at 50-32, their best mark since 1974-1975.

Michael was the scoring champ again with a 35.0 average. During the season he scored more than 40 points in 16 games and bested the 50-point barrier four times. After the season he was named the league's Most Valuable

Player and also Defensive Player of the Year. It was the first time one player had won both awards the same year.

In addition, he was first team All-NBA and a first team All-Defensive choice. About the MVP award, he said, "Winning this award has always been one of my biggest goals. A lot of people see me as just a scorer. This year I was determined to show my all-around game."

In the 1987-1988 play-offs, Chicago beat Cleveland in the first round before losing to Detroit in five games in round two. But the team was getting better. Before the 1988-1989 season the Bulls traded power forward Charles Oakley to the New York Knicks. In return, the team got 7-foot-1 (216-centimeter) center Bill Cartwright. Cartwright was a veteran who knew how to play the game. He wouldn't be pushed around.

And before that same season, Michael Jordan signed a new contract. It was an eight-year deal worth $25 million. The Bulls felt he was worth every penny. The team finished the year at 47-35 as Michael took another scoring title with a 32.5 average. In the play-offs, the Bulls made it all the way to the conference finals where they were beaten by the Detroit Pistons in six games. They were getting closer.

By this time, Michael was one of the most popular athletes in the country. He couldn't go anywhere without being mobbed by fans. But he still found time to visit sick children in hospitals and work for the "Just Say No To Drugs" program and other charities in the Chicago area.

He even once gave his own Air Jordan sneakers to a kid he saw hanging around the streets, on the condition that the boy promise to go back to school. He did, and was given the sneakers.

When Michael's mother heard the story, she said that she wasn't surprised. "Michael is all about giving back."

CHAMPIONS AT LAST

By 1989-1990, Michael and the Bulls felt it was time to get over that last hurdle. It was time to win it all. The club had another good rookie in guard B. J. Armstrong from Iowa. And they also had a new coach in Phil Jackson.

Michael scored 54 points, to the joy of a sellout crowd at Chicago Stadium in the Bulls' first game of the year. Every game the Bulls played that year—home and away—would be a sellout. That's because Michael was now known by all as the most exciting player of his time.

But it was winning that meant the most to him. The team finished second to the Detroit Pistons in the division with a 55-27 record. Once more they made it all the way to the conference finals, only to have Detroit turn them away again. This time it took the full seven games. The Pistons went on to become NBA champs for the second straight year.

Michael was his usual brilliant self. He won his fourth straight scoring title with a 33.6 per game average. As usual, he was an All-Star and on the All-Defensive team. But there was still that one more hill to climb.

In 1990–1991 the team was a year older and a year better. This time, the Bulls put it all together. They finished the regular season with a 61-21 record, good enough to win the Central Division title by 11 games over Detroit.

Michael's great leaping ability can be seen as he takes a jump shot over Johnny Newman of the New York Knicks during 1988 action. Because he could jump so high, even taller players rarely got a chance to block his shots.

Michael was the NBA scoring leader for the fifth straight year. This time he averaged 31.5 points a game. He had help from Pippen and Grant, who were both now at star level.

Then, during the early rounds of the play-offs, Michael was named the league's Most Valuable Player for the second time. When he was handed the trophy at halftime of a play-off game, he asked all his teammates to come out and be with him.

"It was a very touching moment for me," he said. "I've always wanted to simply be part of a team, and the way my teammates have played gives me the feeling of a real family situation."

Now the Bulls went after their remaining goal—the NBA championship. In the first two rounds they defeated the Knicks and the Philadelpia 76ers. And they did it with a real team effort. Next came the Eastern Conference finals and once again the tough Detroit Pistons.

But this time it was different. The Bulls ran the Pistons off the court in four straight games and advanced to the championship round against the Los Angeles Lakers. The Lakers were led by their longtime superstar Magic Johnson. It promised to be a tough series.

The Lakers surprised everyone by winning the first game in Chicago, 93-91. But after that it was all Bulls. Led by Michael, the Bulls swept the next four games to become world champions! It was truly a team victory, and the leader of the team was without a doubt Michael Jordan.

The 1990-1991 season was the year the Bulls finally reached the top. Led by Michael, Chicago marched through the playoffs to win its first NBA championship. In second-round action against the Philadelphia 76ers, Michael maneuvers toward the hoop as the Sixers' Hersey Hawkins tries to stop him.

Michael was the Most Valuable Player in the finals. He averaged 31.2 points, 6.4 rebounds and 10.4 assists. After the game he fell to his knees and hugged the championship trophy.

"It was a seven-year struggle for us," he said. "We started from the bottom, but every year we worked harder and harder until we got it. This means so much to the team and to the city of Chicago."

It had been a real struggle for the Bulls to reach the top. Michael had grown with the team, and many were now calling him one of the best players in NBA history. As soon as the excitement of winning died down, Michael and his teammates set their next goal—to repeat as champions.

REPEAT AND THREE-PEAT

There was no reason to believe the Bulls wouldn't have a great chance to win the championship again. Michael was at the top of his game at age 28. Both Pippen and Grant had become outstanding players. And there were solid role players like center Bill Cartwright, guards B. J. Armstrong and John Paxson, and center/forward Stacey King.

So it was no surprise when the Bulls produced a brilliant regular season. The team finished at 67-15, the best record in the entire league. In fact, they were ten games better than the next best team.

Michael took a sixth straight scoring title. But his 30.1 average was the lowest of the six. That's because the Bulls had a more balanced offense than before. There were more players who could put the ball in the hoop, so the fact that Michael didn't score quite as much didn't mean his game had diminished. His all-around game was more brilliant than ever, and he was rewarded with a second straight Most Valuable Player award. It was also the third of his career. Then Michael and the Bulls started after their second straight NBA championship. This time nearly everyone expected the Bulls to win.

They began with an easy 3-0 sweep of the Miami Heat. In those three games Michael averaged an amazing 45.0 points a game. Next came the very tough New York Knicks. This was a best-of-seven series, and the Knicks played the Bulls close to a standoff. It came down to a seventh and deciding game. Chicago won that one easily, 110-81, to advance to the Conference finals.

There, the Bulls whipped the Cleveland Cavaliers in six games to once again move into the finals. This time the Bulls met the Portland Trail Blazers, a high-scoring team. But the Blazers were no match for Michael Jordan and his teammates.

The Bulls won in six games to take their second straight NBA title. And to the surprise of no one, Jordan was the star. In six games he averaged 35.8 points a game and was once again the finals MVP. Now there was talk of a third straight title and maybe even more than that.

Before the 1992-1993 season began, Michael and teammate Scottie Pippen were part of the "Dream Team"—a team of NBA superstars allowed to play in the Olympics for the first time. Joining the two Chicago stars were Magic Johnson, Larry Bird, Patrick Ewing, David Robinson, Charles Barkley, and others.

It was no surprise when the Americans rolled over everyone to win a gold medal. It was a fun experience for Michael and the team, but it was also tiring. It didn't give the players much of an off-season. Some wondered if Jordan and Pippen would tire during the next NBA season.

That's when talk of a "Three-Peat" began. No team had won three NBA titles in a row since the Boston Celtics of 1964-1966. The Bulls, however, would happily settle for three in a row.

It would not be an easy year for Michael or his teammates. The club was winning again, but not with the ease of the year before. They weren't dominating other teams. In the eyes of many, the Bulls were not a sure bet to win again. They would really have to work for it.

There were problems with the offense. Michael and Scottie Pippen wanted to run more. After that was resolved, Coach Jackson complained that Michael was taking too many shots. He was looking for the balanced scoring of the year before. But Michael had always done what he felt was necessary to win.

"I knew it was going to be tough this year," Michael said, "but frankly it's been tougher than I thought. We're physically and mentally tired, and we're a little out of sync from time to time. But I think we'll be fine when we see the sight of a challenge in the play-offs."

The Bulls won their division with a 57-25 record, 10 fewer wins than the season before. As usual, Michael was the scoring champ. He captured his seventh straight scoring title with a 32.6 average. That tied a record set by Hall of Famer Wilt Chamberlain. Now it was time for Michael and the Bulls to try for that third straight championship—a three-peat.

In the first two rounds, it looked easy. The Bulls topped Atlanta in three straight and then rolled over a tough Cleveland team by winning four in a row. Now they had to meet the Knicks for the Conference championship.

When the Knicks won the first two games at Madison Square Garden in New York, chances for the three-peat seemed to be slipping away.

But the Bulls rebounded to win game three, 103-83. Then in game four, Jordan simply took over. Playing with his usual fire and brilliance, he just exploded for 54 points, hitting six three-pointers along the way as the Bulls won, 105-95. Bulls' guard John Paxson said in admiration: "Night after night, year after year, he just carries this team. He never avoids it, never shirks from it."

Chicago then won the fifth game, 97-94, with Pippen leading the way, and next took the sixth, 96-88, to close the Knicks out. The Bulls had won the series, 4-2, and would now face the Phoenix Suns and Charles Barkley for the NBA crown.

Chicago opened with a 100-92 victory at Phoenix in the first game of the series, with Michael netting 31 points.

"It's all about history now," he said. "We're here to make history."

That's just what the Bulls did. They outplayed the Suns for almost the entire series, wrapping it up in six games. In the final game, John Paxson hit a clutch three-pointer with seconds left to give Chicago a 99-98 victory and a third straight title.

As for Michael, he had been absolutely brilliant. He set another record by averaging 41.0 points for the six-game final. That included a 55-point explosion in game five. And for the third straight year he was named the Most Valuable Player for the finals. But it was the three-peat that meant the most to him.

"It's something I was looking forward to because it separates myself from Magic and Bird."

Michael was referring to the two other great players of his generation—Magic Johnson and Larry Bird. Magic led the Lakers to five titles and Larry led the Celtics to three. But neither team had won three straight.

In a sense, the third title almost put a cap on Michael's career. He was now the most popular and recognizable athlete in the world. And nearly everyone was calling him the greatest ever to play the game.

TRAGEDY AND A NEW LIFE

It was expected that Michael would have a quiet off-season, get a good rest, and then try to lead his team to a fourth straight title. But in July 1993, a news report from North Carolina said that Michael's father, James, was missing. He had been traveling by car on a business trip and had not contacted his family in several days.

As more time passed, the entire nation began to follow the story. Several weeks later, James's car was found abandoned. Shortly afterward, his body was found in a creek. He had been shot to death. Within days, two 18-year-old boys were arrested and charged with shooting James Jordan to death on July 23. While napping in his car along a North Carolina highway, he had been killed in a random robbery. The killers apparently had no idea who he was until they went through his belongings.

Michael soared above everyone in the 1992-1993 finals against Phoenix. Not only did he lead the Bulls to a third straight title, but he also set a record by averaging 41.0 points in the six-game final series.

Michael and his family were devastated by the tragic news. The entire family had been very close. Michael always thought of his father as his best friend. The two men even looked very much alike.

The funeral was kept private and no one really knew how the tragic murder would affect Michael's life and career. Michael himself expressed his grief, but said little else. Then on October 6, just a short time before the Bulls' training camp opened, the team called a news conference. Michael then stepped to the podium and shocked the entire sports world.

He announced to a stunned audience that he was retiring from basketball.

"I have nothing more to prove in basketball," Michael said. "I have no more challenges to get motivated for. It has nothing to do with my father's passing. I have achieved everything in basketball I could . . . My father saw my last basketball game and that means a lot."

Michael also said he wanted to leave while he was on top. He didn't want to be pushed out or not be able to do the things he had once done on the court.

The question was, what would he do next? Some felt he was too young and too competitive to just walk away. He would either have to find another challenge or he would come back. Maybe he just needed a year off to sort things out. Either way, he had compiled an incredible record.

In nine years he had scored 21,541 points, for a career average of 32.3 points a game. That was the highest in NBA history. In 111 play-off games he averaged 34.7 points, also the best ever. Then there were the seven scoring titles, three Most Valuable Player awards and, most important, the three NBA championships. He had truly done it all.

After the tragic murder of his father, Michael shocked the sports world by retiring from basketball. He made the announcement to a packed house of news people with his wife, Juanita, at his side.

But his quiet life of retirement didn't last long. In January 1994, there was another news conference with Michael Jordan as the star. This time Michael announced that he had signed a contract with the Chicago White Sox. He was going to try to become a major league baseball player.

It sounded like an impossible task. Michael hadn't played real baseball since his early high school years. And no one just goes out and becomes an instant major leaguer.

"This is something that has been in the back of my mind for some time," Michael said, "and something my father and I talked about often. I'm very serious about it and feel I've got to give it a try."

Some felt that Michael might have a chance because he was such a great athlete. But most thought it was too late to chase a new dream. He was 31 years old and would undoubtedly have to start in the minor leagues. Michael said he wanted to be treated like everyone else and wasn't looking for a shortcut.

"If my skills aren't at a certain level," he said, "then I won't be a baseball player and won't stay on the field."

In his first public workouts he didn't look good in the batting cage. His swing was long and awkward. He didn't drive the ball with any real sting. Most experts felt he didn't have much of a chance to become a good hitter. But in the outfield he showed some potential, and he was fast on the bases.

During spring training with the White Sox he had just 7 hits in 42 at bats for a .166 batting average. It was finally decided he would play the 1994 season with the Birmingham [Alabama] Barons of the Southern League. That was at the Double-A minor league level, not even the highest level in the minors.

"I've never been afraid to fail," Michael said. "I think I'm strong enough as a person to accept failing, but I can't accept not trying."

So Michael went to Birmingham where the team rode to games in buses, sometimes for up to twelve hours at a time. One of the richest athletes in history was being paid $850 a month to play baseball, ride in a bus, and get $16 a day meal money. He did, however, purchase a new luxury bus in which he and his new teammates traveled.

Michael started in right field for the Barons on April 8. In his first game he struck out twice and hit a weak fly out. He looked good in the outfield, but it was apparent that hitting would be his greatest challenge.

The hitting just didn't come. For most of the season Michael was batting below .200. That isn't good. He was striking out too much and showed very little power for a player his size.

"It's been embarrassing and frustrating," he said, at one point. "And it can make you mad. I've been working too hard at this to make myself look like a fool."

That part was true. Michael was working just as hard as he ever had in basketball. He more than kept up with the 18- and 21-year-old kids who also wanted to make the majors. But he didn't have the time they had.

When the season ended, Michael had a .202 batting average. That wasn't good enough. He hit just three home runs and drove home 51 runs. He certainly did not

Although Michael's form at the plate looks good here, it was his inability to improve as a hitter that ultimately helped end his short baseball career. Ironically, the quickest player in basketball had a "slow bat."

look like a power hitter. He stole 30 bases, but he struck out more than 100 times. Again, the guesswork started about what he would do next.

After the season, Michael returned to Chicago to play in a charity basketball game. It was the last game ever played in old Chicago Stadium. The Bulls would have a new arena in 1994.

Playing with and against many of the top stars in the NBA, Michael showed all his old skills and electricity. He topped all scorers with a 52-point performance. Even though it was a fun game, he showed everyone that he was still special on the basketball court. But he also said he wouldn't be returning to the Bulls. He would give baseball still another chance.

"I went through a lot of changes this year very quickly," he said. "I had a lot of information thrown at me. Overall, I thought I came a long way."

So Michael played baseball in the Arizona Fall League from October to December 1994, just as the NBA season was getting started. But when spring training for 1995 began, the major league players were still on strike. The strike had started August 12, 1994, and caused the World Series to be canceled.

Michael didn't want to be a strike breaker and play in the White Sox exhibition games. He felt he was caught in a bad spot, and early in March he left the White Sox camp. A few days later he showed up at a Bulls practice session. That's when the rumors started. Would he come back to basketball?

On March 10, Michael announced he was retiring from baseball. Then just eight days later, he captured headlines all over the country when he announced he was returning to the Bulls, even though there were just 17 games left in the season.

Once again there was excitement everywhere he went. In his first game the next night against the Indiana Pacers, Michael came out with a new uniform number. Since his number 23 had been retired, he was now wearing number 45, which he had also worn in baseball. He scored 19 points in his first game, hitting on just 7 of 28 shots. But in his fourth game, he scored 32 against Atlanta, and hit the winning jumper at the buzzer.

Then in the next game against the New York Knicks at Madison Square Garden, Michael lit it up from the beginning. He had 14 of 19 field goals and 35 points by halftime. When the game ended, the Bulls had a 113-111 victory and Michael had scored 55 points. It was the most points scored in the NBA season up to that time. Michael Jordan was surely back.

The Bulls won 13 of the 17 games Michael played, and finished the year at 47-35. Michael averaged 26.9 points per game time. It wasn't as good as his career average, but for a player who had been away from the game for 18 months, it was amazing. As the NBA playoffs began, Michael was concentrating on his next goal. "I want to win another NBA championship very badly," he said.

In the first round of the playoffs (a best-of-five), the Bulls had to meet the Charlotte Hornets. The Hornets were led by young superstars Larry Johnson and Alonzo Mourning. But the Jordan-led Bulls handled them in four games, winning the series 3-1.

Michael was up to his old tricks in the opener. The game went into overtime and the Bulls won it, 108-100. Michael had scored 48 big points: He was still capable of the great offensive explosion.

Then in the conference semifinals, Michael and the Bulls went up against the Orlando Magic. The Magic were led by center Shaquille O'Neal. They also had former Bull Horace Grant as power forward. Many felt the two big men would be too strong for Chicago.

Michael rejoined the Bulls at the tail end of the 1994-1995 season. For several games he wore a new number (45) before returning to number 23. In just his fifth game back he scored an amazing 55 points against the New York Knicks.

In game one, Michael had a rare bad night. He scored just 19 points. Worse than that, he had 8 turnovers and made several mistakes in the final minutes. Orlando won, 94-91. It was disappointing, but Michael stepped forward to say, "I take the credit and I'm willing to take the blame, too."

Then, before game two, Michael suprised everyone. He came onto the floor at Orlando wearing his old uniform number 23. He said it was a last-minute decision but that he would stick with the old number for the rest of the series. "Twenty-three is just me," Michael said, and then went out and scored 38 points as the Bulls won 104-94.

Not even the number change could help the Bulls in the long run. Orlando was too strong and won the final two games to take the series in six, 4-2. It was a disappointing finish for Michael and his teammates. In 10 play-off games, Michael had scored 315 points for a 31.5 average. It was a few points below his career play-off average, but still outstanding.

In the eyes of most, Michael's comeback was very successful. To be away from the game for so long and to play so well was truly amazing. He has already said he will be back for a full season in 1995-1996. His goal, as always, will be to help his team win another championship.

Michael Jordan has always had the need to win, and he has always looked for more and greater challenges. Maybe he needed time away from basketball so he could eventually come back and prove once again that he's still the greatest. Almost everyone agrees that he is the best and most exciting individual talent ever to play the game.

"If I lost my talent tomorrow, I'd say I had a great time and move on. I live for today but plan for the future," Michael has said.

He moved away from basketball once, played baseball, and then came back to the hardwood. Now he says he's going to stay awhile because he realizes all over again how much he loves it. As his former archrival Magic Johnson once said, "There's Michael, and then there's everybody else."

MICHAEL JORDAN: HIGHLIGHTS

1963	Born on February 17 in Brooklyn, New York.
1978	Enters Laney High School in Wilmington, North Carolina.
1981	Enters University of North Carolina at Chapel Hill. Named to starting Tar Heel team.
1983	Named to All-Star teams. Named College Basketball Player of the Year.
1984	Again named Player of the Year. Tar Heels win ACC title. Plays for U. S. Olympic gold-medal basketball team. Signs with NBA Chicago Bulls.
1985	Named to Eastern division All-Star squad. Named NBA's Rookie of the Year. Named Rookie of the Year by the *Sporting News*.
1987	Wins the NBA scoring title with 3,041 points.
1988	Wins the NBA scoring title; named NBA MVP. Named NBA Defensive Player of the Year.
1989	Wins the NBA scoring title.
1990	Wins the NBA scoring title.
1991	Wins the NBA scoring title; named NBA MVP and NBA MVP of the finals. Bulls win the NBA championship.
1992	Wins the NBA scoring title; named NBA MVP and NBA MVP of the finals. Bulls win the NBA championship.
1993	Wins seventh straight NBA scoring title; named NBA MVP of the finals. Bulls win NBA championship. Surprises sports world by retiring from basketball at age 30.
1994	Announces he has signed a baseball contract with the Chicago White Sox. Plays 1994 baseball season with Birmingham Barons in the minor leagues. Plays in the Arizona Fall League.
1995	Leaves baseball and returns to basketball. Averages 31.5 points in 10 play-off games to complete his comeback year.

FIND OUT MORE

Beahm, George. *Michael Jordan: A Shooting Star.* Kansas City, MO: Andrews & McMeel, 1994.

Dolan, Sean. *Michael Jordan, Basketball Great.* New York: Chelsea House, 1994.

Knapp, Ron. *Michael Jordan: Star Guard.* Hillside, NJ: Enslow Publishers, 1994.

Lipsyte, Robert. *Michael Jordan: A Life Above the Rim.* New York: HarperCollins Children's Books, 1994.

Raber, Thomas R. *Michael Jordan: Basketball Skywalker.* Minneapolis, MN: Lerner, 1992.

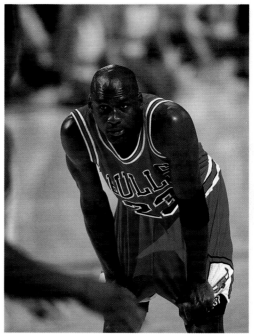

How to write to Michael Jordan:

Michael Jordan
c/o Chicago Bulls
One Magnificent Mile
980 N. Michigan Avenue, Suite 1600
Chicago, IL 60611

INDEX